NAVY

John Townsend

EDGE

W

FRANKLIN WATTS

LONDON·SYDNEY

This edition 2014

First published in 2013 by
Franklin Watts
338 Euston Road
London NW1 3BH

Franklin Watts Australia
Level 17/207 Kent Street
Sydney NSW 2000

A CIP catalogue record for this book is available from the British Library.

Dewey number: 940.5'41

(PB) ISBN: 978 1 4451 2629 6
(Library eBook) ISBN: 978 1 4451 2570 1

Printed in China

Franklin Watts is a division of Hachette Children's Books,
an Hachette UK company.
www.hachette.co.uk

Series editor: Adrian Cole
Editor in Chief: John C Miles
Art direction: Peter Scoulding
Design: Simon Borrough
Picture research: Diana Morris

Acknowledgements:
Bettmann/Corbis: front cover.
DEA/De Agostini/Getty Images: 5.
GeoEye: 20.
The Granger Collection/Topfoto: 17.
Hulton Archive/Getty Images: 7.
MPI/Getty Images 29.
National Archive/HIP/Topfoto: 4.
Picturepoint/Topham: 9, 27t.
Popperfoto/Getty Images: 11, 13.
2nd Class William G Roy/US Navy: 21.
Topfoto: 1, 6, 8, 10, 27b.
ullsteinbild/Topfoto: 18, 28.
US Naval Historical Center: 16.
US Navy: 12, 19, 23, 24t, 24b, 26.
courtesy of ussubvetsofwwII.org: 22.
Wikipedia: 14, 25.

Every attempt has been made to clear copyright. Should there be any
inadvertent omission please apply to the publisher for rectification.

Contents

War at Sea   4

Hitler's Navy   6

The Royal Navy   8

Case Study:
Battle of the River Plate   10

Battleships   12

Case Study:
The *Bismarck*   14

Japan Attacks   16

The US Navy   18

Case Study:
Battle of Midway   20

Subs in the Pacific   22

Aircraft Carriers   24

Destroyers   26

Final Naval Battles   28

Timeline   30

Glossary   31

Index   32

War at Sea

During the 1930s Adolf Hitler and his Nazi Party became the ruling power in Germany. By 1939 it was clear that Germany planned to take over Europe. When German forces invaded Poland, Britain and France warned Hitler to stop. He refused and war was declared. Other countries soon became involved as World War II spread.

THE
BRITISH NAVY
guards the freedom of us all

This Royal Navy recruiting poster shows how important navies were during World War II.

During the six years of World War II, thousands of ships manned by millions of sailors formed a constantly alert action force on the oceans around the world. The many sea battles they fought had a major impact on the outcome of the war.

Each navy had two main tasks:
- to attack enemy targets (eg ships, ports, shore installations in other countries)
- to defend its own shores from attack, as well as protect sea-lanes and friendly shipping. Also to ferry troops from place to place.

Sunk! A direct hit on an Allied warship sends it to the bottom.

AF FACTS

World War II lasted from 1939 to 1945 and involved 61 countries.

25 million people in all armed forces were killed; many more were injured.

Allies: forces fighting against Germany and Japan, such as France, Britain and the USA

Axis: the armed forces of Germany, Japan, Italy and others

ACTION STATS

Size of German, British and French navies in 1939 (full time staff)

German navy   78,000 (approx)

Royal Navy   120,000 (approx)

French navy   160,000 (approx)

Hitler's Navy

Hitler was Commander-in-Chief of the *Kriegsmarine* — the German navy from 1935 to 1945. Although its navy was smaller than its enemies, Germany had great plans for building a far superior naval force. This was called 'Plan Z', which aimed to create a fleet of 800 ships manned by 200,000 men.

The Kriegsmarine's most lethal ships were its U-boats ('undersea boats' or submarines). For the first few years of the war, U-boats attacked Allied ships carrying supplies across the North Atlantic Ocean.

U-boats hunted in groups called 'wolf-packs', and fired torpedoes (underwater missiles). These tactics sank thousands of Allied ships during what became known as the Battle of the Atlantic. Allied navies had to find ways of striking back at U-boats.

The ensign (ship's flag) of the Kriegsmarine flying on a German U-boat.

German U-boats travelled on the surface before submerging to avoid detection and to attack.

ACTION STATS

At the beginning of World War II (WWII), the German navy had only 55 U-boats. During the war it built another 1,150. In the Battle of the Atlantic, U-boats sank over 2,600 ships while the Allies sank almost 800 U-boats. Of the 40,000 men who served on U-boats during WWII, 30,000 never returned. This was the highest casualty rate of any armed service in the history of modern warfare.

AF FACTS

On 3 September 1939, a U-boat fired a torpedo and sank the British liner SS *Athenia* without warning – against the rules of war. Over 100 passengers were killed, but Hitler said the Kriegsmarine was not responsible.

The Royal Navy

During World War II Britain imported about half its food and all its oil by sea. It needed a strong naval force to protect merchant ships transporting these vital supplies from North America and elsewhere. Much of the Royal Navy's efforts were directed towards protecting the critical North Atlantic sea routes from attack.

The Royal Navy used fast and agile escort vessels to attack U-boats.

ACTION-STATS

At the start of World War II, the Royal Navy operated more ships than any other. By the end of the war, the US Navy had become the world's largest.

In 1939 the Royal Navy had 15 battleships, 7 aircraft carriers, 66 cruisers, 184 destroyers, 45 escort and patrol vessels and 60 submarines. Many more of each type were completed during the war.

AF FACTS

Not all the Royal Navy's efforts were directed at U-boats. In May and June 1940 it provided critical cover when thousands of British and French troops had to be evacuated from Dunkirk in France.

Canada and the USA helped the Royal Navy by providing escort vessels to protect convoys (groups) of merchant ships from the deadly U-boats. From August 1941, these ships used radar which could detect a U-boat periscope at a range of two km. And in 1942 the U-boat *U-559* was captured with an 'Enigma' coding machine and code books on board. This key information helped the Allies track U-boats and attack them.

Nazi Germany invaded France in May 1940. A huge fleet of both small civilian ships and Royal Navy vessels evacuated more than 300,000 Allied troops from Dunkirk under constant attack from German aircraft.

Case Study: Battle of the River Plate

The Battle of the River Plate was the first major naval battle of World War II. Three of the Royal Navy's ships (HMS *Exeter*, *Ajax* and *Achilles*) took on the mighty German 'pocket battleship' *Admiral Graf Spee,* which was sinking merchant shipping off the coast of South America.

ACTION STATS

Admiral Graf Spee
- Weight: 14,890 tons
- Length: 186 metres
- Max speed: 29.5 knots
- Range: 16,500 km at a speed of 20 knots
- Armament: 6 x 28-cm guns, 8 x 15-cm guns, 6 x 10.5 cm guns, 4 x 3.7-cm guns, 10 x 2-cm guns, 8 x 53-cm torpedo tubes and two Arado Ar196 aircraft

In December 1939, the four ships engaged in a famous battle in the River Plate estuary in South America. The massive guns of the *Graf Spee* scored hits on all three British ships. HMS *Exeter* was badly damaged. The Royal Navy's smaller guns failed to penetrate the *Graf Spee*'s 14-cm-thick steel armour, until finally a shell damaged the ship's fuel system.

Opposite: the Graf Spee *on fire and sinking after the battle.*

The *Graf Spee* limped into the neutral port of Montevideo where the captain decided to destroy his ship rather than let the Allies seize it. The captain wrote a letter to Hitler, then killed himself. The end of the *Graf Spee* was celebrated by the Allies as their first real naval victory of the war.

Light cruiser HMS Ajax, which took part in the Battle of the River Plate.

Battleships

Battleships were the largest and most powerful warships of each navy. They had the thickest armour and huge firepower from large-calibre guns. Battleships were the leading vessels of each naval fleet and rarely operated alone. They were protected by faster, smaller ships.

AF FACTS

World War II began and ended with battleships. In 1939, the German battleship *Schleswig-Holstein* fired the first shots of the war as Nazi troops invaded Poland.

On 2 September 1945, the final surrender of the Japanese Empire took place aboard the battleship USS *Missouri*, officially ending World War II.

A group of US battleships, pictured in 1945 at the end of World War II.

When enemy fleets met, the battleships would form a 'line of battle' and manoeuvre to maximise the number of guns that could fire.

After the destruction of the *Graf Spee*, the pride of the German navy was the *Tirpitz* — one of the most modern battleships of the war. With armour over 30 cm thick and massive firepower, this was a battleship the Allied navies had to take seriously. Eventually, in 1944, she was sunk by British aircraft. Huge aerial bombs exploded the battleship's own ammunition and she rolled over and sank, trapping more than 1,000 men inside.

ACTION STATS

Tirpitz
- Weight: 42,900 tons
- Length: 251 metres
- Max speed: 30 knots
- Range: 16,400 km at a speed of 19 knots
- Armament: 8 x 38-cm guns, 12 x 15-cm guns, 16 x 10.5-cm AA (anti-aircraft) guns, 16 x 3.7-cm AA guns, 8 x 53.3-cm torpedo tubes and four aircraft
- Crew: 2,400

This photo shows the Tirpitz *anchored in a fjord in Nazi-occupied Norway. She was found and sunk by Royal Air Force bombers.*

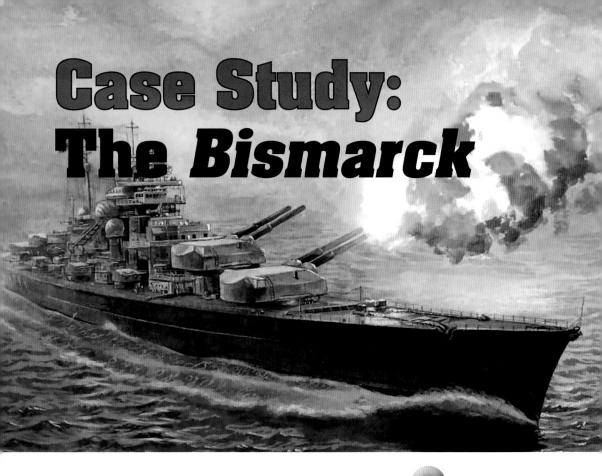

Case Study: The *Bismarck*

The sinking of two great warships in 1941 brought an end to the age when battleships were the major forces in naval warfare. Submarines and aircraft carriers took over as the key vessels in the war at sea.

 This painting shows the Bismarck *firing its main guns.*

The sister ship of the *Tirpitz* was the *Bismarck* – one of Germany's most famous battleships of World War II. It was a formidable ship. The Royal Navy sent HMS *Hood*, its prize battleship, to attack it in the North Atlantic. *Bismarck* fired its massive guns, smashing a shell through *Hood*'s deck. A huge explosion tore the ship in half and it sank in minutes. All but three of the 1,419 crew were lost.

ACTION STATS

Bismarck

Launched in 1939

Armament:

- 8 x 38-cm guns
- 12 x 15-cm guns
- 16 x 10.5-cm AA guns
- 16 x 3.7-cm AA guns
- Four Ar196 aircraft

HMS _Hood_

Launched in 1918

Armament (1941):

- 8 x 15-in guns
- 14 x 4-in AA guns
- 24 x 2-pounder guns
- 20 x .5-in machine guns
- 4 x 21-in torpedo tubes

After this disaster the Royal Navy sent a large force to attack the _Bismarck_. Heavy gunfire from battleships HMS _Rodney_ and _King George V_ hammered the _Bismarck_ until it was ablaze. Finally, HMS _Dorsetshire_ fired three torpedoes, and the _Bismarck_ sank with the loss of more than 2,000 men.

AF FACTS

The Royal Navy was able to sink the _Bismarck_ because the German battleship's rudder had been smashed by a torpedo fired by a plane from aircraft carrier HMS _Ark Royal_. The _Bismarck_ was a sitting duck.

Battleship HMS Hood, _sunk by the_ Bismarck _in 1941._

Japan Attacks

In the 1930s, Japan built up one of the world's largest navies. This enabled it to invade Malaya and the East Indies for their oil and rubber. However, Japan feared the US might try to stop its plans so it attacked the US Pacific Fleet.

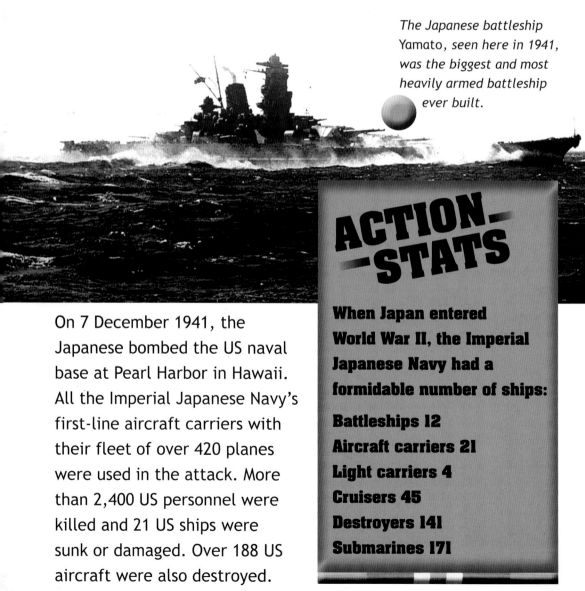

The Japanese battleship Yamato, *seen here in 1941, was the biggest and most heavily armed battleship ever built.*

On 7 December 1941, the Japanese bombed the US naval base at Pearl Harbor in Hawaii. All the Imperial Japanese Navy's first-line aircraft carriers with their fleet of over 420 planes were used in the attack. More than 2,400 US personnel were killed and 21 US ships were sunk or damaged. Over 188 US aircraft were also destroyed.

ACTION STATS

When Japan entered World War II, the Imperial Japanese Navy had a formidable number of ships:

Battleships 12
Aircraft carriers 21
Light carriers 4
Cruisers 45
Destroyers 141
Submarines 171

Until the attack on Pearl Harbor, the US had not joined World War II — other than giving naval support for Allied merchant shipping. Suddenly the USA was forced into the war and within days, other Axis nations declared war on the United States. The Pacific Ocean was set to become a major arena for naval battles with the mighty Imperial Japanese Navy.

AF FACTS

When it came to tonnage of warships in World War II, the Imperial Japanese Navy was the second most powerful navy in the Pacific (after the US). That made it the third-largest navy in the world (after the UK and the USA).

Battleship USS West Virginia *burned and sank after being hit with seven aerial torpedoes in the attack on Pearl Harbor.*

The US Navy

After the attack on Pearl Harbor, the US Navy had to recover quickly and engage in the war against Japanese expansion in the Pacific. The first chance they had to do this was in May 1942 at the Battle of the Coral Sea. This was the first naval battle where the enemies fired without their ships coming within sight of one another. Japan, until then seemingly unstoppable, had now been checked.

ACTION STATS

The US Navy's aircraft carriers operated in the Pacific so that US planes could more easily attack Japanese forces. With 4,500 pilots and 3,400 planes, the US had more airpower than the Japanese navy.

YOUR NAVY – FIRST LINE OF ATTACK

NAVY DAY OCT. 27TH

After the USA entered the war, thousands of sailors were needed to man its ships. Posters like this one helped find recuits.

New ships had to be built fast, and the USA had the money and manpower to do just that. By 1945, hundreds of new US ships were in operation, including 18 new aircraft carriers and 8 new battleships — a total of 6,768 ships by the end of the war.

Four huge *Iowa* class battleships were launched to defend the fleet and attack Japanese targets in the Pacific Ocean. USS *Iowa* had fearsome firepower but one of its first missions was to take US President Franklin Roosevelt to an Allied conference in Casablanca, North Africa, in 1943.

USS Iowa *remained a part of the US Navy until 1990. This photo shows the ship firing its huge guns during an exercise in 1984.*

Case Study: Battle of Midway

Six months after the attack on Pearl Harbor, the US Navy defeated Japan in one of the most important naval battles of World War II. The Battle of Midway in June 1942 crushed Japan's naval strength when four of its aircraft carriers were destroyed. The Imperial Japanese Navy never fully recovered from its defeat at Midway.

The US fleet had a naval base on the small Midway Islands in the North Pacific Ocean. The Japanese navy set out to ambush the fleet, then take over the base. US intelligence had already discovered this plan so its ships were prepared and waiting.

The fierce battle that followed destroyed four of the Japanese navy's vital aircraft carriers but only one US aircraft carrier — USS *Yorktown*. Although the US base at Midway was damaged by an air attack, it remained operational and played a vital part in the USA's eventual success in the Pacific.

This aerial photo of the Midway Islands shows the runways of the US base.

ACTION STATS

Casualties and losses:

USA
- 1 aircraft carrier sunk
- 1 destroyer sunk
- 150 aircraft destroyed
- 307 killed

Japan
- 4 aircraft carriers sunk
- 1 cruiser sunk
- 248 carrier aircraft destroyed
- 3,057 killed

AF FACTS

After being hit several times and attempts at saving it had failed, the *Yorktown* finally capsized and sank on 7 June 1942. The wreck was found in 1998.

Smoke pours from USS Yorktown *after being hit in the boilers by Japanese dive bombers at Midway.*

Subs in the Pacific

World War II submarines were surface ships that could travel underwater for only a short time. Diesel engines gave them a high speed and long range on the surface. However, speed and range were very limited below the surface. This was because the batteries that powered the sub underwater needed regular recharging by surfacing to run the air-breathing diesel engines.

ACTION STATS

USS *Balao*
- Weight: 1,550 tons
- Length: 95 metres
- Crew: 80
- Armament: 1 x 4-in deck gun, 1 x 40-mm AA gun, 10 x 21-in torpedo tubes with 24 torpedoes
- Max speed: 20 knots
- Max speed (submerged) just under 9 knots
- Cruising speed: 10 knots
- Range: 20,000 km surfaced at a speed of 10 knots

Balao could stay submerged for 48 hours.

USS Balao, pictured on the surface with some of its crew on deck.

Japanese midget submarines fill a Tokyo dockyard after the war.

Submarines formed less than two per cent of the US Navy, but sank over 30 per cent of Japan's navy, including eight aircraft carriers. US subs also crippled the Japanese economy by sinking almost five million tons of shipping — over 60 per cent of Japan's merchant ships.

However, there was a high cost — 314 submarines served with the US Navy in the war, most of these being sent to the Pacific. Fifty-two US submarines never returned, nor did 3,505 sailors. This was the highest percentage of men killed in action of any US force in World War II.

AF FACTS

Midget submarines operated by a crew of one or two were used by navies in WWII. Japan also used suicide midget submarines as well as suicide scuba divers who would swim under boats with explosives on bamboo poles — to destroy both the boat and themselves.

Aircraft Carriers

The success of aircraft carriers during World War II meant that many navies concentrated their efforts on building this important vessel.

ACTION STATS

USS Franklin
- **Weight: 27,100 tons**
- **Length: 266 metres**
- **Max speed: 33 knots**
- **Range: 37,000 km at 15 knots**

Armament:
- **8 x 5-in guns in twin mountings,**
  4 x 5-in guns in single mountings,
  32 x 40-mm AA guns in quad mountings,
  46 x 20-mm guns in single mountings

Aircraft:
- **90–100 aircraft**
- **Crew: 2,600**

The mighty Franklin *steaming in the Pacific, its flight deck crowded with aircraft.*

The wings of most carrier aircraft folded to save space. This is the USS Essex *pictured in March 1943.*

Japan's massive carrier Shinano *remains the largest ship ever sunk by a submarine.*

An aircraft carrier's main function was to act as a seagoing airbase. Each carrier had over one thousand sailors and over 30 aircraft. The US Navy had more than 90 carriers during the war, Japan about 30 and the Royal Navy had 24.

The USS *Franklin*, nicknamed 'Big Ben', was one of 24 *Essex*-class aircraft carriers built during World War II as the backbone of the US Navy's combat fleet. Entering service in 1944, it served in campaigns in the Pacific. The ship was badly damaged by a Japanese air attack in March 1945, with the loss of over 800 of its crew. USS *Franklin* was the most heavily damaged United States carrier to survive the war.

AF FACTS

Apart from being the largest carrier built at the time, the Imperial Japanese Navy's *Shinano* (above) was the shortest-lived carrier in WWII. On its maiden voyage in November 1944, it was torpedoed by the USS *Archer-Fish*, a *Balao*-class submarine. It kept sailing but lost power and, after eleven hours, the huge ship capsized with all its 1,350 crew.

Destroyers

When torpedoes were developed in the late 1800s, navies realised they needed small, fast warships to protect their fleets. These 'torpedo-boat destroyers' were smaller than cruisers and, by World War II, had become known simply as 'destroyers'.

USS McGowan *was a Fletcher-class destroyer. It was launched in 1943 and saw extensive service during World War II and afterwards.*

This picture shows a torpedo being launched from a ship.

Destroyers became essential for attacking torpedo-firing submarines and preventing them from getting in range to attack cruisers, battleships or aircraft carriers. They also had to prevent enemy destroyers closing in to strike with torpedoes, as well as scouting waters for submarines or mines, often close to shore.

Many ships were badly damaged when hitting enemy mines (floating bombs) in the sea. Some mines were dropped by aircraft. Others were anchored unseen just below the surface. Navies also used destroyers to drag a device that sliced through the mine's mooring line. The mine would float to the surface where it could be shot at and exploded safely. Another method used electrical cables to pass pulses of electricity through the water to blow up the mine.

AF FACTS

Torpedoes are self-propelled weapons with an explosive warhead. They can be fired above or below the water but travel at speed towards the target, detonating on contact or nearby. By the end of World War II, some torpedoes were fitted with guidance systems to make them 'home in' on the sound waves coming from the target.

A direct hit explodes a floating mine, protecting other ships from danger.

Final Naval Battles

Battles in the Pacific Ocean continued to the very end of World War II. As the war in Europe was coming to an end, the USA was preparing for a major sea battle to win the war against Japan. This turned out to be one of the biggest naval conflicts of all, with huge loss of life.

Deadly threat - a Japanese kamikaze suicide pilot crashes his bomb-laden plane into a US ship during the final stages of the war in the Pacific.

The battle for the island of Okinawa, to the south of Japan, in April 1945, was a bloodbath. More than 7,000 US personnel were killed on land and 5,000 were lost at sea. More than 32,000 were wounded. The Japanese lost 107,000 men and 7,400 were taken prisoner. Although 16 Japanese ships were sunk compared to 36 US ships, Japan lost 4,000 aircraft as well as its most powerful battleship, the *Yamato*. Nearly all its sailors were killed.

The last Allied ship sunk by enemy action in World War II was a submarine — USS *Bullhead*. This was on 6 August 1945, the day the US attacked the Japanese city of Hiroshima with the first atomic bomb. Eight days later World War II was over.

AF FACTS

In Europe, Allied troops finally closed in on Berlin in April 1945 and the Nazi Third Reich was defeated. Hitler killed himself and Germany surrendered. VE (Victory in Europe) Day was celebrated on 8 May 1945. Japan finally surrendered three months later on 14 August 1945.

Japanese officials sign the instrument of surrender aboard USS Missouri *on 2 September 1945.*

World War II Timeline

Some of the key naval events of World War II

1939 1 September: World War II begins
September–onwards Battle of the Atlantic
December Battle of the River Plate

1940 25 May–4 June: Evacuation of forces from Dunkirk
November Battle of Taranto in the Mediterranean

1941 May: Sinking of HMS *Hood* and *Bismarck*
7 December Japanese attack USA at Pearl Harbor

1942 May: Battle of the Coral Sea — Pacific
June: Battle of Midway — Pacific
October: *U-559* sunk; Enigma machine and naval
codebooks captured

1943 September: Operation Jaywick — Pacific
December: Battle of the North Cape — Atlantic Ocean

1944 6 June: D-Day — Invasion of Nazi-occupied France
by Allied forces
June: Battle of the Philippine Sea — Pacific
August: German Battleship *Tirpitz* sunk

1945 March-June: Battle of Okinawa — Pacific
14 August: Japan surrenders; World War II ends

Glossary

AA guns – anti-aircraft guns

Allies – countries (US, Britain and its Empire, Soviet Union) opposing the Axis forces

Axis – countries (Germany, Italy, Japan) opposing the Allies

battery – a set of big guns that are controlled as a unit

battleship – the biggest warships of World War II, with the largest and heaviest guns

calibre – the diameter of a gun barrel and the shell it fires. German naval guns were described in metric measurements (eg. 38 cm); British and US guns were described in Imperial measurements (eg. 15 in)

cruiser – a large fast warship smaller than a battleship but larger than a destroyer

destroyer – a fast warship smaller than a cruiser and armed with torpedos; used for anti-submarine and escort duties

knot – one nautical mile per hour (1.85 kilometres or 1.15 miles)

Kriegsmarine – the navy of Nazi Germany in World War II

maiden voyage – very first journey or mission

merchant ship – any ship carrying civilian supplies and armed only for self-defence

mine – an anti-ship bomb that floats just under the surface and explodes on contact

neutral – not joining either side in a conflict

periscope – an instrument that allows crew members in a submarine to see above the surface of the water

personnel – people employed for a task, such as in the navy

torpedo – an underwater missile launched by a submarine or a destroyer

U-boat – German submarine - 'undersea boat'

Index

Admiral Graf Spee 10, 11, 13
aircraft carriers 9, 14, 15, 16, 18, 19, 20, 21, 23, 24–25, 27

Battle of Midway 20–21
Battle of Okinawa 28
Battle of the Atlantic 6, 7
Battle of the Coral Sea 18
Battle of the River Plate 10-11
battleships 9, 10, 12-15, 16, 17, 19, 27, 28
Bismarck 14–15
British navy see Royal Navy

convoys 8–9
cruisers 9, 10, 11, 12, 16, 21, 26, 27

destroyers 9, 16, 21, 26-27

Enigma machine 9

French navy 5, 6, 13

German navy 5, 6-7, 10, 11, 12, 13

guns 10, 11, 12, 13, 14, 15, 19, 22, 24

HMS Achilles 10
HMS Ajax 10, 11
HMS Ark Royal 15
HMS Dorsetshire 15
HMS Exeter 10, 11
HMS Hood 14–15
HMS King George V 15
HMS Rodney 15
Hitler, Adolf 4, 6, 7, 11, 29

Imperial Japanese Navy 16, 17, 18, 20, 23, 25

Kriegsmarine 6-7 see also German navy

merchant ships 8, 9, 10, 17, 23
mines 27

Pearl Harbor 16–17, 18, 20
Pacific Ocean 16-19, 20–21, 23, 24, 25, 28

Royal Navy 4, 5, 6, 7, 8–11, 13, 14, 15, 17, 25

SS Athenia 7
Schleswig-Holstein 12
Shinano 25
submarines 6, 9, 14, 16, 22–23, 25, 27, 29
submarines, midget 23

Tirpitz 13, 14
torpedoes 6, 7, 10, 13, 15, 17, 22, 25, 26–27

U-boats 6, 7, 8, 9
U-559 9
US Navy 9, 12, 13, 16, 17, 18–25, 26
USA 5, 9, 16, 17, 19, 28, 29
USS Archer-Fish 25
USS Balao 22
USS Bullhead 29
USS Essex 24, 25
USS Franklin 24, 25
USS Iowa 19
USS McGowan 26
USS Missouri 12, 29
USS West Virginia 17
USS Yorktown 20, 21

Yamato 16, 28